YORK NOTES

An Inspector Calls

J.B. Priestley

Notes by John Scicluna

 Longman   York Press

YORK PRESS
322 Old Brompton Road, London SW5 9JH

ADDISON WESLEY LONGMAN LIMITED
Edinburgh Gate, Harlow,
Essex CM20 2JE, United Kingdom
Associated companies, branches and representatives throughout the world

First published 1997

ISBN 0–582–31327–9

Designed by Vicki Pacey, Trojan Horse
Illustrated by Susan Scott
Typeset by Pantek Arts, Maidstone, Kent
Phototypeset by Gem Graphics, Trenance, Mawgan Porth, Cornwall
Produced by Longman Asia Limited, Hong Kong
Colour reproduction and film output by Spectrum Colour

CONTENTS

PREFACE

York Notes are designed to give you a broader perspective on works of literature studied at GCSE and equivalent levels. We have carried out extensive research into the needs of the modern literature student prior to publishing this new edition. Our research showed that no existing series fully met students' requirements. Rather than present a single authoritative approach, we have provided alternative viewpoints, empowering students to reach their own interpretations of the text. York Notes provide a close examination of the work and include biographical and historical background, summaries, glossaries, analyses of characters, themes, structure and language, cultural connections and literary terms.

If you look at the Contents page you will see the structure for the series. However, there's no need to read from the beginning to the end as you would with a novel, play, poem or short story. Use the Notes in the way that suits you. Our aim is to help you with your understanding of the work, not to dictate how you should learn.

York Notes are written by English teachers and examiners, with an expert knowledge of the subject. They show you how to succeed in coursework and examination assignments, guiding you through the text and offering practical advice. Questions and comments will extend, test and reinforce your knowledge. Attractive colour design and illustrations improve clarity and understanding, making these Notes easy to use and handy for quick reference.

York Notes are ideal for:

• Essay writing
• Exam preparation
• Class discussion

The author of these Notes is John Scicluna, who, having studied English and Drama, began teaching in 1967. Since that time he has been actively involved in the teaching of English and English Literature to secondary age pupils.

The text used in these Notes is the Heinemann Plays edition, 1992, with an introduction and notes by Tim Bezant. Page numbering is the same as in the earlier Hereford edition.

Health Warning: **This study guide will enhance your understanding, but should not replace the reading of the original text and/or study in class.**

PART ONE

INTRODUCTION

HOW TO STUDY A PLAY

You have bought this book because you wanted to study
a play on your own. This may supplement classwork.

- Drama is a special 'kind' of writing (the technical
  term is 'genre') because it needs a performance in the
  theatre to arrive at a full interpretation of its
  meaning. When reading a play you have to imagine
  how it should be performed; the words alone will not
  be sufficient. Think of gestures and movements.

- Drama is always about conflict of some sort (it may
  be below the surface). Identify the conflicts in the
  play and you will be close to identifying the large
  ideas or themes which bind all the parts together.

- Make careful notes on themes, characters, plot and
  any sub-plots of the play.

- Playwrights find non-realistic ways of allowing an
  audience to see into the minds and motives of their
  characters. The 'soliloquy', in which a character
  speaks directly to the audience, is one such device.
  Does the play you are studying have any such
  passages?

- Which characters do you like or dislike in the play?
  Why? Do your sympathies change as you see more of
  these characters?

- Think of the playwright writing the play. Why were
  these particular arrangements of events, these
  particular sets of characters and these particular
  speeches chosen?

Studying on your own requires self-discipline and a
carefully thought-out work plan in order to be effective.
Good luck.

J.B. PRIESTLEY'S BACKGROUND

Priestley's experience of working-class life.

John Boynton Priestley was born on 13 September 1894 and was raised in a modest but thoroughly middle-class home in Bradford, Yorkshire, where his father was a schoolmaster. J.B. Priestley was proud of the fact that his grandparents had been mill workers, and his childhood home was certainly a place where socialist ideals thrived. In *Rain upon Godshill* (1939) he wrote of his visits to 'grandparents and uncles and aunts who still lived in the wretched little "back-to-back" houses in the long, dark streets behind the mills' which gave him real experience of working-class life and people. The effect of these early influences comes across in many of his plays where, as in *An Inspector Calls*, he exposes exploitation and oppression.

His writing career begins after his time as a soldier and a student.

He left school at sixteen and took a job with a firm of wool merchants. During the First World War he joined the 10th Duke of Wellington's Regiment and served on the front line in France. He was buried alive and injured when a trench collapsed, and was later gassed and invalided home. He never forgot the terrible things that he saw during that war. In 1919 he was given an ex-serviceman's grant and studied Modern History and Political Science at Trinity Hall, Cambridge. He married Pat Tempest, a young woman he had met in Bradford, in 1921, and on leaving Cambridge worked as a freelance writer and a reader for the publishing company Bodley Head. His articles in the *Times Literary Supplement* earned him a good reputation which was enhanced by the publication of *The English Comic Character* in 1925. That same year his wife died of cancer. The following year he married Jane Wyndham Lewis, with whom he had been having an affair during Pat's illness, and by whom he had had a daughter, Mary, while Pat was still alive. Despite numerous affairs his marriage to Jane lasted for twenty-six years. After this he married the writer Jacquetta Hawkes.

Y

J.B. Priestley wrote seven books which were a mixture of semi-autobiographical and travel writings (some as a result of visits to America, Egypt and the Sudan), seven volumes of social history and over twenty novels, of which *The Good Companions* (1929) was his first big success. Two years later J.B. Priestley worked with Edward Koblock to produce a play version of *The Good Companions*, and during the thirties and forties he concentrated on writing plays. He wrote, or co-wrote, some forty plays in all, many of them giving clues to his socialist beliefs. His travels through some of the poorer parts of Britain in 1934 were the basis for *English Journey* which helped him to focus on his political ideas and to refine them.

After success in other forms of writing he begins writing plays.

An Inspector Calls was written in 1945 in just one week. J.B. Priestley had the gift of writing quickly and is said never to have corrected his first drafts. He would shut himself away, face away from the window and plug his ears with cotton wool to ensure concentration! During the Second World War he managed to write fourteen books and to broadcast a radio programme called *Postscripts* each Sunday evening. While these programmes were popular with the listeners who liked his blunt but friendly personality, his Yorkshire accent and his often romantic way of putting things, combined with his habit of criticising the government and commenting on what he thought was wrong with society, led the BBC to stop them after about a year.

J.B. Priestley was very interested in politics, but seemed to have trouble settling down with the policies of any one political party. He made an unsuccessful attempt to stand for Parliament as an Independent candidate in 1944, and in 1945 he visited the Soviet Union where *An Inspector Calls* had its first production. He became an active supporter of the Campaign for Nuclear Disarmament but turned his back on it when he felt it was attracting too radical a group of people. His sort of socialism, later in his life we could say liberalism, was based on compassion – the sort of compassion and caring that the Inspector wants to see in those he questions in *An Inspector Calls*.

Note Priestley's views on the playwright's job.

Most of his plays are about middle-class people, partly because theatre audiences were generally middle class and so could easily identify with the characters, and partly because J.B. Priestley believed that a writer should create characters and situations based on his own experience. J.B. Priestley generally wanted his characters to be as real as possible, so he provided them with a clearly recognisable social background, an appropriate environment and some elements of a past life.

J.B. Priestley became very interested in theories about time. His interest was sparked by *A New Model of the Universe* written in 1931 by P.D. Ouspensky, and by two books written by J.W. Dunne – *An Experiment with Time* (1927) and *The Serial Universe* (1934). In *An Inspector Calls* we see J.B. Priestley's interpretation of Ouspensky's theory that existence is a cycle of lives from which we can only escape if we change for the better, a change which we can only make with the help of a particularly gifted or extraordinary person (see Theme on Time). His plays *Dangerous Corner* (1932), *Eden End* (1934) and *Time and the Conways* (1937) all contain important elements of time theories which suggest that, in our lives, there are important moments when the decisions we make can lead us towards either disaster or salvation.

J.B. Priestley died in 1984.

Industrial setting

The setting of *An Inspector Calls* is important in a number of ways. J.B. Priestley sets the play in the industrial city of Brumley. This is not a real place but one that the playwright has invented – perhaps using his memories of his own childhood in the industrial city of Bradford. Brumley is probably typical of many towns where the factory owners, who provided much needed employment, were able to run things pretty much as they wanted. Although it is a fictional place, J.B. Priestley gives us quite a lot of information about it.

The Burlings are seen to live in an unequal society.

The importance of the town is indicated by its having a Lord Mayor and a police force with its own Chief Constable. A visit by a member of the Royal Family is mentioned, and Arthur Birling clearly feels that his activities in local politics and his being Lord Mayor at the time of the visit will have made him enough of a figure to justify his being given a knighthood. The number of women who are poor and in need of help is suggested by the existence of the Brumley Women's Charity Organisation with which Mrs Birling is involved. Such organisations, which relied upon the financial support of rich people, were frequently found in large industrial towns and cities during the Victorian and Edwardian periods. It is interesting to notice that whether someone got help or not could depend on whether the organisers, like Mrs Birling, thought that person deserved to be helped or whether they thought that the person deserved to suffer.

As well as the wrongs done by the Birling family, we are told of the behaviour of Alderman Meggarty. This suggests that J.B. Priestley was making a general point that the family were not the only ones whose actions had a destructive effect on others, and so we get a picture of a time when the underprivileged and powerless are made the victims of the privileged and powerful. By setting the play before the First World War, J.B. Priestley could make the most of these social divisions.

Priestley's use of stage and set

All action of the play takes place in the Birling's dining room, which is described as 'substantial and heavily comfortable, but not cosy and homelike', and though the family enjoy an outwardly respectable and comfortable way of life, their relationships are not cosy and tensions lurk within them. The realistic stage set has another function. J.B. Priestley liked to begin his plays by convincing his audiences that they were safely within the boundaries of what was real and normal – and then he would find a way to destroy that feeling of reality and move them into an unreal or mysterious situation. By using the solid and naturalistic stage setting he created that sense of reality while the mysterious role of the Inspector and the time-switch at the end of the play introduce the unreal elements.

The influence of money and social status

The social and historical context of the play are equally important. Social position was far more important than it is today. Following the dramatic expansion of industry throughout the nineteenth century, many men who had invested in such industries as coal, iron and steel, pottery and textiles had made considerable fortunes. Men such as Arthur Birling may have come from humble origins but their wealth allowed them to rise up the social ladder. Marriages between these newly rich families and aristocratic, but often impoverished land-owning families, helped to secure new social positions. Many of these industrialists were granted titles and this too helped to improve their social standing. The Labour Party, founded by James Keir Hardie in 1893, was only just beginning to make an impact on the political life of the country. The rights of workers, like Eva Smith, were not taken too seriously by many employers, but at the same time many working

Some employers were generous while others were selfish.

people had benefited from the generosity of those industrialists who genuinely cared for the welfare of their workers, even to the extent of building idealistic new towns for them to live in. Men like Arthur Birling could be seen as a throwback to harsh early Victorian times, but sadly he may have been all too typical of the greedy employers of that time. Life might have been good for him, but it was not good for his workers. Although King Edward VII died in 1910, the time from his accession to the throne in 1901 and the start of the First World War in 1914 is usually referred to as the Edwardian Era. To many people, and J.B. Priestley may have been such a person, the end of the Edwardian era and the onset of the war marked an end to a time of peace and stability, and harking back nostalgically to it can be a sort of escape from an unpleasant and uncertain future. Yet the Edwardian era was a period of false security. In his play *Eden End* which he also set in 1912, J.B. Priestley has one of his major characters say 'the world's got a lot more sense than it's given credit for in the newspapers. And it's got science to help it'. J.B. Priestley wrote *Eden End* in 1934 and there is a clear message against the complacent attitude that so many were showing towards the rise of the dictators in Germany, Italy, Spain and the Soviet Union. Similarly in *An Inspector Calls*, Mr Birling looks to a prosperous future without wars, a future where technology will bring progress unspoiled by social problems.

The First World War brought important social changes.

Just as in 1934 when J.B. Priestley was warning against the rise of European dictators, so in 1945 (when *An Inspector Calls* was actually written) he is warning of the consequences of not making the social changes that natural justice demanded. J.B. Priestley had fought in the First World War and had seen the soldiers, who had been promised that they would return to a 'fit country for heroes to live in' (David Lloyd George,

1918), returning home to the grim reality of
unemployment, recession, strikes and hunger marches.
He would surely have wanted something more
worthwhile and honourable when the new Labour
government with its promise of a Welfare State swept
to victory after the horrors of the Second World War.

IMPORTANT HISTORICAL EVENTS BETWEEN 1910 AND 1945

1910 Edward VII dies
The murderer, Dr Crippen, is the first criminal
suspect to be caught as a result of a radio message
First demonstration of motion picture with
sound
Pure Radium isolated by Marie Curie

1911 James Ramsay MacDonald elected leader of the
Labour Party

1912 White Star liner *Titanic* sinks with loss of over
1500 lives

1914 Assassination of Archduke Franz Ferdinand
sparks off First World War

1915 German submarine sinks Cunard liner *Lusitania*,
killing some 1400 passengers including 128
American citizens

1917 Tsar Nicholas II abdicates as rebellion grows in
Russia
America declares war on Germany and joins
allies

1918 Kaiser Wilhelm II abdicates and Armistice ends
the war
Representation of the People Act gives married
women over 30 the right to vote

1919 Alcock and Brown complete first non-stop
transatlantic flight

1920 League of Nations has its first meeting
Coal miners strike throughout Britain

1921 Irish Free State created as a British dominion

1922 Irish Republican Army shoots Field Marshal Sir
    Henry Wilson in London
    Mussolini leads his Fascists on Rome
1923 German currency collapses
1924 First Labour Government formed under Ramsay
    MacDonald
1926 General Strike hits British industry
1928 Equal Franchise Act gives vote to all women
    aged 21
1929 American economy hit by slump and Wall Street
    crash
1931 Rising unemployment in United Kingdom leads
    to protests, strikes and hunger marches
1933 Hitler, leader of Nazi Party, elected Chancellor of
    Germany
1936 King George V dies. Edward VIII becomes king,
    but abdicates, before his coronation, less than a
    year later
1939 German invasion of Poland leads to outbreak of
    Second World War
1940 Battle of Britain
1941 Germany attacks Russia, and Japan attacks
    American fleet at Pearl Harbour. Russia and
    America join allies
1944 Allied armies invade Europe – D-day
1945 Hitler commits suicide; Germany surrenders
    Atomic bombs dropped on Hiroshima and
    Nagasaki lead to surrender of Japan and end of
    Second World War
    Churchill's wartime government resigns
    Labour Government formed under Clement
    Attlee
    An Inspector Calls has its first showing in Moscow

Part two

Summaries

General summary

Act I

Mr Birling, his wife and their grown-up children, Eric and Sheila, have been enjoying a family dinner celebrating the engagement of Sheila Birling to Gerald Croft. In an expansive mood, Mr Birling makes pompous speeches outlining his views on technology and industrial relations. He says that a man only needs to care for himself and his family and that they should ignore the 'cranks' who claim that everybody has a responsibility to care for everybody else in the community. The evening is interrupted by the arrival of a police inspector named Goole making enquiries about the suicide of a young woman, Eva Smith.

The Inspector begins to draw members of the Birling family into his enquiries about the girl's death.

Shown a photograph of the girl, Mr Birling admits he had employed her in his factory some two years previously but had sacked her for being one of the leaders of a strike for higher wages. Gerald Croft supports Birling's claim that he had acted reasonably, while Sheila and Eric both feel that their father acted harshly in sacking her. When Sheila is also shown the photograph she realises that, driven by jealousy and ill-temper, she later had the same girl sacked from her job as a shop assistant.

The Inspector appears to have an uncanny knowledge of the family's dealings with Eva Smith. When he announces that the girl had changed her name to Daisy Renton, Gerald's reaction makes it clear that he too had known the girl. By the end of the act the Inspector has begun to suggest that many people share a joint responsibility for the misery which prompted Eva Smith/Daisy Renton to end her sad young life. Sheila warns Gerald not to try to conceal anything from the Inspector.

Act II	The strain of the earlier part of the evening is evident in the tension between Sheila and Gerald. Gerald admits that in the spring of the previous year he had met Daisy Renton and she had become his mistress. He had ended the affair some six months later. Sheila is hurt and angry at Gerald's involvement with the girl, yet she feels a certain respect for the openness of his admission.
Further revelations about the girl deepen the family's involvement with the case.	Despite Mrs Birling's attempts to intimidate the Inspector and to control events, Sheila's feeling that it is foolish to try to hinder his enquiries appears increasingly well founded. Sheila is concerned that her mother will also be implicated in the girl's suffering. While Eric is out of the room, despite her blustering, Mrs Birling is forced to admit that just two weeks earlier the girl had tried to get help from Mrs Birling and had been refused. It is revealed that the girl was pregnant and there is now a strong suspicion that Eric might have been the father of that unborn child.
Act III	Eric confesses that he had got the girl pregnant. He had also stolen money from his father's firm to try to support her. Eric is horrified to learn that his mother had refused to help the girl and he blames his mother for the death of the girl and of the unborn child. Any pretence at family unity starts to dissolve. The Inspector has done his job and shown that each of them had a part in ruining the girl's life. He makes a dramatic speech about the consequences of the sort of social irresponsibility that Mr Birling had been preaching at the end of the dinner, and he leaves.
The Inspector's strange behaviour leads to doubts about his identity.	Between them Gerald and Mr Birling are gradually able to prove that the man was not a real police inspector. This raises a doubt about whether they have really all been talking about the same girl – and about whether any girl had actually killed herself. A telephone call to

The play's ending suggests that the Birling family's problems are far from over.

the Infirmary confirms that there is no record of any girl dying there that afternoon. There is a general feeling of relief at this information. Sheila and Eric still feel guilty for their actions and they seem to have been changed for the better by what has happened. The others feel a greater sense of relief; their confidence and belief in the rightness of their actions is restored. At this point the telephone rings. Mr Birling answers it to find that it is the police calling. He is told that a young woman has just died on her way to the Infirmary and an inspector is on his way to make enquiries into her death.

Y

ACT I

PART ONE

[pp. 1–7]

Consider what we learn of Mr Birling's attitudes towards marriage and society.

In his stage directions (see Literary Terms), J.B. Priestley takes care to set the scene in the large house of a wealthy business man. He briefly describes the four members of the Birling family and their guest, Gerald Croft. A meal celebrating the engagement of Gerald Croft to Sheila Birling is just ending. The port is passed round and glasses are filled for a toast to the happy couple. Mr Birling makes a speech congratulating the engaged couple and expressing the hope that their marriage will lead to closer and more profitable links between the firms owned by the Birling and Croft families. The toast is drunk, and Gerald chooses his moment to present Sheila with an engagement ring. Birling continues his speech, emphasising his confidence that the future will bring good times to manufacturers like them with fewer strikes and greater prosperity. He talks about advances in technology, quoting the newly launched *Titanic* as a symbol of progress. He says that by 1940 the world will be a place of peace and prosperity, with strikes and wars as things of the past. He says it is important for sensible business men to speak out against socialist ideas. Mrs Birling, Sheila and Eric leave the dining room.

COMMENT

The solid and substantial house, the champagne glasses, decanter of port and the cigars reflect the comfortable, rich lifestyle of the well-respected Birling family.

The easy, light hearted conversation shows Sheila as excitable, youthful and enthusiastic, while Eric seems shy, awkward and close to getting drunk. Gerald appears self-assured and someone who knows how to behave at all times. Mrs Birling takes little part in the conversation and what she does say reinforces the idea that she is a cold person who stands apart from others. Mr Birling, by

Think about how
Mr Birling's
certainty in his
opinions colours
our view of him.

contrast, is in a good mood but cannot resist making speeches. His comments show how wrong he can be: the Titanic would sink on its maiden voyage; there would be two World Wars; depression, social unrest, unemployment and strikes would characterise the next three decades.

GLOSSARY   **chump** a light-hearted way of calling someone a fool

steady the Buffs a way of suggesting that someone needs to take care. The expression is found in Kipling's *Soldiers Three* and refers to a British Army regiment, later called the Royal East Kent Regiment

Capital Birling uses the word to represent those who owned the factories

The Balkans the geographical region comprising Greece, Bulgaria and the states of the former Yugoslavia. That part of the world has frequently been a trouble spot. It was the shooting of Grand Duke Ferdinand in Sarajevo which sparked off the First World War, and more recently we have seen war break out there following the break-up of Yugoslavia

the *Titanic* famous passenger liner built for the White Star Line in Belfast. It was claimed to be unsinkable, but on its maiden voyage it struck an iceberg and sank on 14 April 1912 with the loss of some 1500 lives

Bernard Shaw and H.G. Wells both of these famous writers had an interest in social justice and the socialist cause – as did J.B. Priestley himself

Labour Birling refers here to employed working people rather than the political Labour Party

PART TWO
[pp. 7–11]

Look at how Mr Birling seems to be closer to Gerald than to his own son.

Gerald remains in the dining room with Mr Birling who expresses his concern that Gerald's mother, Lady Croft, fears that the Birling family are socially inferior to the Crofts. To put Gerald's mind at ease, Birling confides that there is a strong possibility that he will be knighted in the next Honours List. They are joking that a public scandal could prevent Birling from getting his knighthood as Eric enters. Eric is not let into their secret. As he has another drink Eric reports that Mrs Birling has asked them not to be too long over the port, though, as the women are talking about clothes there is little real urgency.

Birling lectures Gerald and Eric on a man's responsibility being to himself and to his family. He is warning them not to have anything to do with ideas of 'community and all that nonsense' when he is interrupted by the doorbell and the announcement that Inspector Goole has arrived. Birling and Gerald make light-hearted remarks about how awkward it would be if Eric had 'been up to something', and Eric appears unnerved by their jokes.

COMMENT   Apart from the superiority that Sir George has because of his title, Lady Croft's family come from the land-owning gentry. Birling is clearly concerned that his place in society depends on his acquired wealth rather than on good family connections.

Birling sees a knighthood as a fair reward for his involvement in local politics as well as a way for him to become an equal of Sir George Croft.

J.B. Priestley shows us how superficial the honours
system can be when Birling's faithful support of a
political party counts so highly towards his gaining a
knighthood. Birling is happy to accept the community's
reward in the form of a knighthood, but his speech
shows that he regards real commitment to the
community as being nonsense.

It is particularly striking that the family's feeling of self-
satisfaction shown by Birling's comments about
responsibility coincide with the moment of the Inspector's
arrival. This is ironic (see Literary Terms) since the
Inspector is there to try to teach them all something about
the real responsibility they have towards other people.

GLOSSARY   **useful party man** one who supports a political party and is loyal
to its policies
cranks colloquial word meaning people who hold strange ideas
or views

Part three

[pp. 11–16]   The Inspector is shown in. Birling tries to take control,
carefully mentioning his long service in local
government and his position as a magistrate. The
Inspector refuses to be impressed and explains that he
has come to make enquiries about a girl who has died
in the Infirmary after deliberately drinking disinfectant.
Birling cannot see how this matter can involve him.

Notice how
Priestley
introduces the idea
of events in time
being like links in
a chain.

The Inspector tells him the girl's name and shows him
a photograph of her. Birling remembers he had
employed the girl, Eva Smith, in his factory but had
sacked her for her part in leading a strike for higher
wages. The Inspector declares that even though he had
sacked the girl nearly two years ago, Birling had still
been a link in the chain of events leading to her death.
Gerald supports Birling's view that it was right to sack
the ring-leaders. Eric feels his father acted harshly,

Compare Mr Birling's attempt to intimidate the Inspector with the way Mrs Birling behaves in Act III (pp. 30–1)

especially as Birling admits the girl was a good worker who had been considered for promotion. Birling is irritated by Eric's apparent lack of business sense, and by the Inspector's insinuations, and tries to use his friendship with the Chief Constable to frighten the Inspector. The Inspector remains calm and determined. Birling shrugs off responsibility for the girl's death but is curious as to what happened to her after she had been sacked from the factory.

COMMENT

The Inspector is represented as being an incorruptible force for good. He is described as creating a big impression and as being solid and purposeful. His control of the situation and his sincerity contrast sharply with Birling's attitudes.

Birling's relaxed and condescending manner becomes aggressive as he finds himself having to defend his actions.

Birling is a hard-headed businessman who considers that his importance in local politics, his role as a magistrate, his social position and influential friends make him superior to a mere police inspector.

Birling has no sense of loyalty towards his workers. He regards the strike with contempt and refuses to consider the workers' need for more money if it means he must have less profit. Birling admits that Eva Smith had good qualities, she was lively and a good worker, but he disliked her willingness to voice her opinions. Gerald's support of Birling shows that he too cares more for profits than for the welfare of those his company employs.

List the information given about Eva Smith.

Eva Smith does not appear, yet she is central to the developing action of the play. Since J.B. Priestley makes her case through the Inspector, who is a sympathetic character, we feel he too is sympathetic towards her. She has left a diary and a letter which give the Inspector all his leads.

GLOSSARY   **alderman** senior member of a town council
              The Bench collective term for local magistrates
              warrant document signed by a magistrate which allows the
              police to search or arrest a suspect
              Infirmary hospital
              twenty-two and six predecimal currency used pounds, shillings
              and pence. There were twenty shillings to every pound. The six
              refers to six pence, which was half a shilling
              twenty five shillings as above. This sum was equal to £1.25
              Chief Constable the senior officer in charge of a county or
              municipal police force
              public-school and varsity Eric had had the privilege of being
              educated in a fee-paying school and of going to university
              go on the streets become a prostitute

PART FOUR

[pp. 16–21]

Sheila, bringing a request that the men join the ladies in the drawing room, interrupts the conversation. Birling thinks that their business with the Inspector is ended, and he is annoyed when the Inspector shows that he wants to continue his enquiries and that he wants Sheila to stay. Sheila is shocked when the girl's suicide is described. Birling again ridicules the idea that his sacking of the girl two years earlier could have had any link to her death. Eric feels there might be a connection and Sheila feels sympathy for the girl, but Gerald again supports Birling's view.

Look at how Sheila reacts to the girl's suicide and imagine how she feels when she sees the photograph.

The Inspector implies that others might know something of the girl's life and Birling becomes less aggressive. He senses a possible scandal and, wishing to avoid any public unpleasantness, tries to settle things quietly with the Inspector. Sheila is curious, but the name Eva Smith means nothing to her. The Inspector tells them that she changed her name after she was sacked from Birlings, that she was out of work for two

months and was feeling desperate till she had the good
fortune to find a fresh start working in a dress shop.
She had done well there for a time but a complaint
from a customer had forced her employer to sack her.
This story agitates Sheila. On being shown the
photograph Sheila runs out of the room crying.

COMMENT   The Inspector begins to draw others into the tragedy of
Eva Smith's life and death. He attracts the sympathy of
Sheila and of the audience by his clear and hard-hitting
description of the girl's misery. That sympathy for the
girl is added to by the details of her pleasant
appearance, the poverty she suffered from the loss of
her job at Birlings and by the absence of relatives to
help her when she was in trouble.

Consider the part   The girl is shown to have been a victim of
the Birlings have   circumstance. She lost her jobs at Birlings and at
played in the girl's   Milwards for reasons which J.B. Priestley intends the
misfortunes.   audience to feel were harsh and unjustified.

Sheila's initial distress at having her happy evening
spoiled by the sad news serves to reflect the greater
unhappiness of the dead girl's life and to foreshadow
the greater distress that Sheila will feel when she sees
the photograph.

Through the Inspector's comments on the way that
factory owners exploited the desperation of others, J.B.
Priestley begins to put across his message about social
injustice.

The careful references to the girl getting a job at
Milwards in December (of 1910) and losing it at the end
of January (1911) help to show the timing of events
leading to her suicide. We begin to see that the passing of
time and when things happen are important to the plot.

GLOSSARY   **short-handed** without enough workers

PART FIVE

[pp. 21–6]   Birling is angry with the Inspector for upsetting Sheila. He goes out to tell his wife what is happening. Gerald asks to see the photograph, but the Inspector insists on following his enquiries through in his own way and in his own time. The Inspector suggests that there is sometimes little to chose between respectable citizens and criminals.

Sheila returns and confesses that she was the customer who had had the girl sacked. She admits she had gone to Milwards to buy a dress which did not suit her. The pretty shop girl, whom the dress would have suited, had smiled. Sheila had been angry and jealous. She had complained that the girl had been impertinent and had insisted that the manager get rid of her. The Inspector makes Sheila realise what a terrible thing she had done. He sums up what has so far been revealed about the involvement of Birling and Sheila, and then tells them that after being sacked from the shop the girl had changed her name to Daisy Renton. Gerald reacts sharply to the name.

Think about the way that Sheila's feelings about herself and about Gerald change during the last part of this act.   While Eric takes the Inspector to find Mr Birling, Sheila challenges Gerald. She realises that Gerald's lack of attention to her the previous summer was because he was having an affair with Daisy Renton. Gerald tries to deny it. He then admits he had known Daisy Renton, but says he has not seen her for six months. Sheila advises Gerald not to try to fool the Inspector. The Inspector returns.

COMMENT

Birling is more concerned that his daughter has been upset than by any feelings of guilt or shame for what they might have done to Eva Smith. He does not yet realise the depth of the family's involvement and still feels able to be angry and outspoken towards the Inspector.

The Inspector's comment 'a nasty mess somebody's made of it' shows his increasingly moralistic tone. This leads to his comment 'if it was left to me' which sets him up as a judge, and gives him the authority to state that his enquiries are being made so that all concerned might try to understand why the girl had died.

The Inspector points out Sheila's petty motives of jealousy and anger, and the misuse of her power as the daughter of rich and influential parents to blackmail the shop into sacking the girl. When he tells Sheila she is only partly to blame we realise he intends that all of them should share the responsibility.

Sheila's regret seems genuine. Although the Inspector will not accept belated regrets as an excuse, Sheila has learnt a lesson and she is determined never to act so unfairly again.

Gerald's reaction to the name Daisy Renton is as clear a sign of recognition as was Sheila's earlier reaction to the photograph. He is the only one whose reaction is triggered only by a name which suggests that he had a very close relationship with her. He feels that since he is no longer seeing the girl everything is all right but Sheila has an understanding of the Inspector's power to make them reveal all.

Pick out some moments in Act I that you feel show the Inspector's power over other characters.

Sheila's sense of the Inspector's power and the Inspector's one word question at the end of the act raises the Inspector's position to that of someone who is an all-knowing inquisitor. This adds to our sense of mystery as to where the Inspector has got so much detailed knowledge.

GLOSSARY   **heavy-handed** officious, bullying
a bit thick shocking
tantalus a stand for bottles which has a special lock allowing people to see the bottles but not to remove them without the key
crushed defeated

TEST YOURSELF (Act I)

A *Identify the speaker.* *Ins*

M.B

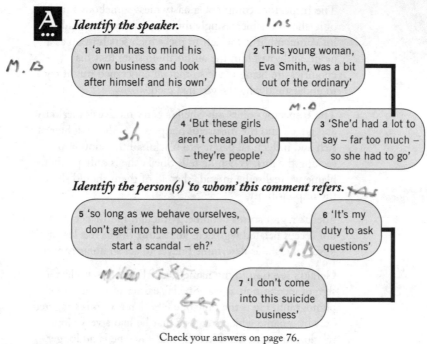

1 'a man has to mind his own business and look after himself and his own'

2 'This young woman, Eva Smith, was a bit out of the ordinary'

M.O

sh

4 'But these girls aren't cheap labour – they're people'

3 'She'd had a lot to say – far too much – so she had to go'

Identify the person(s) 'to whom' this comment refers.

5 'so long as we behave ourselves, don't get into the police court or start a scandal – eh?'

6 'It's my duty to ask questions'

M.B

7 'I don't come into this suicide business'

Check your answers on page 76.

B *Consider these issues.*

a The effect J.B. Priestley creates through the detailed description of the setting given in the stage directions at the beginning of Act I.

b How we are shown the importance Mrs Birling sets on good manners and correct social behaviour.

c The ways that a modern audience would be able to see how wrong Mr Birling was about future events.

d The facts we learn about Eva Smith from Mr Birling's comments.

e The different attitudes towards the rights of ordinary people shown by Mr Birling and by the Inspector.

f The differences in the way that Sheila and Gerald respond to the story of how Mr Birling sacked Eva Smith.

g Why Sheila reacted so strongly to the photograph she was shown.

h Sheila's reaction to the revelation that Gerald had known the girl.

y

ACT II

PART ONE

[pp. 27–9] Gerald resents the decision that Sheila should stay to hear the details of his involvement with Daisy Renton. He suspects that she only wants to see him shamed since he had been there when she made her shameful admissions. The Inspector suggests that that is not the case. He says that Sheila has accepted her share of responsibility and needs to hear what else happened to the girl so that she does not feel she is the only one who is to blame. They agree that sharing something, even blame, is better than not sharing anything. Mrs Birling comes in.

COMMENT Gerald's excuse that Sheila should be spared the ordeal of listening to his story as it might be unpleasant and disturbing for her, is shown to be hypocritical since Daisy Renton had not been spared what was unpleasant and disturbing for her. The argument between Sheila and Gerald reveals a lack of real trust and understanding in their relationship.

Think about the way that Sheila's reactions help us question the identity of the Inspector. The Inspector seems to understand Sheila's feelings in a strange, almost unnatural, way. He does not spare her feelings and his blunt way of describing the circumstances of the girl's death adds to the sense of guilt felt by Sheila and Gerald. At the same time that bluntness increases the sense of condemnation that the audience feels for those who have mistreated the girl.

Sheila is struck by the truth of what the Inspector says, even though she cannot properly understand his power or his nature.

PART TWO

[pp. 29–32]

Contrast Sheila's openness and honesty with Mrs Birling's aloof desire to reveal as little as possible.

Mrs Birling is full of confidence and tries to show the Inspector how superior she is. She suspects that Sheila is only motivated by unhealthy curiosity and has no need to stay and be a part of an enquiry into the life or death of a girl from the working class. She is puzzled when Sheila tries to warn her that the Inspector can break down any defences. Mrs Birling feels that the Inspector's attitude and questioning are offensive and impertinent and she tries to impress him by reminding him of her husband's importance in the community. They discuss Eric's behaviour which Mrs Birling believes has resulted from his not being used to drinking. She is shocked when Sheila, supported by Gerald, reveals that Eric has been drinking far too much for the past two years. She accuses Sheila of being the one who is destroying the family's reputation. Mrs Birling is confident that she can handle any questions which are put to her since she knows nothing about the girl, but Sheila is aware that her mother has not yet faced being questioned by the Inspector. Mr Birling comes in.

COMMENT

Mrs Birling's sense of her social importance gives her a feeling of security which leads her to treat the Inspector with less respect than the others have done. Her superior tone when she comes in is out of keeping with the apprehension which Sheila and Gerald share as a result of their feelings of responsibility.

We are again reminded of Mr Birling's respected position in the community, but Sheila has already realised that outward respectability is no guarantee of sound moral behaviour.

The Inspector recognises that Sheila and Eric are more easily touched by the sadness of the girl's death.

Y

Someone like Mrs Birling, who feels her place in society puts her above such concerns, will clearly be less easily moved.

J.B. Priestley makes a pointed play on words when the word 'offence' is repeated twice each by Mrs Birling and the Inspector. At first it is used to suggest the possibility of someone being offended, but then there is also the suggestion of the law having been broken and an offence taking place.

The revelations about Eric's drinking habits show us how Mrs Birling prefers to conceal the truth, to build up a wall behind which she and her family can hide. It also helps to prepare us for Eric's admissions about his behaviour towards the girl when he was drunk.

GLOSSARY   **girl of that class** working class girl, therefore socially inferior to the Birling family

PART THREE

[pp. 32–40]   Mr Birling, who has been trying to persuade Eric to go to bed, is further annoyed by the Inspector's insistence on doing things his own way. Birling and his wife are startled by the suggestion that Gerald had known Daisy Renton, as the girl was then calling herself. Gerald makes a feeble attempt to deny any link with the girl. He then admits he had met the girl in the bar of the Palace Variety Theatre, a favourite haunt of prostitutes. The girl had seemed different from the other women. She was being pestered by a local dignitary and Gerald

Contrast Gerald's   had managed to rescue her from him. He had taken her
confession with   to a quiet hotel where they had talked. She gave him
Mr Birling's   some vague information about her life and it was clear
earlier   that she was poor and hungry. He had arranged to meet
unwillingness to   her again two nights later and had found her
accept any blame.   somewhere to live. She had then become his mistress.

Birling is angry that his daughter is having to hear
Gerald's story, but the Inspector supports Sheila's right to
hear it. Gerald admits he had been flattered by the girl's
love and admiration but that he was not in love with her.
When he had to go away on business for some weeks he
had taken the opportunity to break off the relationship
and had given the girl some money to live on for a time.
Although Gerald does not know what became of the
girl, the Inspector reveals that her diary showed that she
had gone away to a seaside place to enjoy the memory of

Think about   the happiness she had had with Gerald. Gerald feels the
Sheila's reaction to need to walk in the fresh air after his confession. Sheila
Gerald's confession   gives back his ring. She admits she has been impressed
and how their   by his honesty but feels that after what they have heard
relationship is   about each other they need to get to know each other
affected.   over again. Gerald goes out for a walk.

COMMENT   We are made more aware of the Inspector's ability to
          ask very simple questions and yet to obtain a great deal
          of information.

          Sheila is again seen to be more aware of the Inspector's
          power to make people confess. She is more deeply
          influenced by the girl's story and more conscious of the
          family's responsibility for what has happened.

Sheila becomes increasingly sarcastic with Gerald and this could be her way of coping with the revelations about him.

J.B. Priestley is careful that the men use euphemistic (see Literary Terms) language such as

'... Daisy Renton, with other ideas.'
'Women of the town'

which hints at prostitution without actually mentioning it. To do otherwise would have offended ladies of 1912.

Compared to the 'hard-eyed, dough-faced women', Daisy Renton's prettiness and youth make her seem vulnerable. We are more likely to blame Gerald for what happens, even though we can appreciate his motives for rescuing her from Alderman Meggarty.

Gerald's honest confession helps to add to our knowledge of when things happened to Eva Smith/Daisy Renton. It also makes him a more sympathetic character. Sheila respects his honesty.

The Inspector has already used a photograph to establish the girl's identity, and the 'rough sort of diary' is a convenient device to explain his close knowledge of events.

GLOSSARY   **You needn't give me any rope** to give someone rope is to provide a person with the means by which they can 'hang' themselves, that is do themselves mischief
Stalls bar a bar on the ground floor of a theatre. The stalls of a variety theatre would have been the cheapest seats
Palace Variety Theatre a theatre which had performances of music, comedy, juggling and dance rather than serious plays
haunt meeting place
women of the town prostitutes

PART FOUR

[pp. 40–2]

Think about the way the Inspector uses the photograph and about how reliable it is as a piece of evidence.

Sheila comments that Gerald was not shown the photograph. The Inspector points out that it was unnecessary, and he shows the photograph to Mrs Birling. She claims that she does not recognise the girl, and she is angry when the Inspector says that she is lying. Birling demands an apology from the Inspector who, instead of apologising, points out that power and influence bring responsibilities as well as privileges. Sheila is aware that they must not try to hide behind their respectable reputation. She tells her mother that the Inspector has already got them to admit that the girl had been fired by Birling for asking for a reasonable wage, fired from the shop because Sheila was jealous of her and then taken up by Gerald as his mistress and dropped by him. Sheila advises her mother to tell the truth and not to make things worse. The front door slams and Birling goes to see if Eric has left the house.

COMMENT

Sheila is the only one who appreciates the Inspector's power to reveal their dark secrets. Her summary of what has happened to the girl reminds us of the greed, jealousy and selfishness they have shown. Birling and his wife are still trying to use their sense of power and social status to remind the Inspector of his relatively humble social status. The Inspector shows no fear of Birling's importance in the town. He emphasises the ideas of duty and responsibility to suggest the family's lack of such qualities.

The Inspector's sense of assurance again makes us think that he knows everything and that his questions provide the others with an opportunity to admit their faults. Such an admission, as in Gerald's case, can bring the possibility of forgiveness.

GLOSSARY

Public man someone who is known for his involvement in local government or other important organisations

PART FIVE

[pp. 42–9]

Look at how Mrs Birling's attitude, and language, affect our view of her.

Through his persistent questioning, the Inspector gradually forces Mrs Birling to admit that two weeks ago she had chaired a meeting of the Brumley Women's Charity Organisation. Mr Birling returns with the news that Eric has left the house. The Inspector says that if Eric is not back soon he will go and find him. It is revealed that the girl had appealed to Mrs Birling's organisation for financial help. The girl had called herself Mrs Birling, and this had angered the real Mrs Birling who had used her influence to ensure that the girl had received no help. Mrs Birling feels no regret for what she did, claiming that she had done her duty as the girl had told a pack of lies and so did not deserve help. The Inspector reveals that the girl was pregnant and that Mrs Birling knew this. Mrs Birling had insisted that the child's father should be the one to help. Sheila is appalled by her mother's heartless attitude, while Mr Birling only seems concerned about the possibility of a public scandal.

Mrs Birling now says that the girl knew who the child's father was but that she would not reveal his name. The girl had said that the father had offered to marry her but that she thought he was too immature to take on the responsibility. He had offered her money, which she had refused to take. The Inspector makes Mrs Birling admit that the girl believed the money was stolen and so her refusal to accept it had been justified. Mrs Birling resists the Inspector's attempts to make her feel sorry for the girl's death. She insists that the blame lies with the girl herself and with the child's father. Sheila fears what may be revealed next and tries to stop her mother from saying any more. Mrs Birling goes on to show how she believes the child's father is the chief culprit. She says he deserves to be caught and made to

Consider the ways that Eric fits the description of the father of the unborn child.

publicly admit his guilt. She realises, too late, that her
son Eric is probably the father of the child. The front
door slams and Eric comes in.

COMMENT   The time scale of events leading to the girl's death is
brought almost up-to-date when it is revealed that Mrs
Birling saw her only two weeks before. There is still the
gap between the end of Gerald's affair with the girl and
Mrs Birling's meeting with her.

Mrs Birling has a strong sense of how people of
different classes should behave. Her prejudice, and
dislike of the girl's manner, echo Mr Birling's attitude
when he had said 'She'd a lot to say – far too much – so
she had to go' (p. 15) and Sheila's anger because the girl
had been 'very impertinent' (p. 24). Each had used their
power and position in order to harm the girl.

Mrs Birling's arrogant and snobbish self-confidence is
not dented by anything Sheila says, and only at the end
of the act does she begin to realise that she may have
made a mistake. Her conviction that the father 'should
be made an example of' only serves to set a trap for her
and for Eric.

Mr Birling is becoming increasingly concerned about
the possibility of a public scandal. He is mainly worried
because of the effect it could have on his chances of
getting a knighthood.

The girl has used the name Mrs Birling. We later find
out why she has done this, but Sheila's increasing
agitation, the description of the father and the fact that
Eric is the only one who has not yet been questioned
are all useful clues as to what might happen next.

A

Identify the speaker.

Sheila

1 'You mustn't try to build up a kind of wall between us and that girl'

2 'Nothing but morbid curiosity'

Syb

4 'Yes, I think it was simply a piece of gross impertinence'

3 'You see, we have to share something. If there's nothing else, we'll have to share our guilt'

Identify the person(s) 'to whom' this comment refers.

5 'It's bound to be unpleasant and disturbing'

6 'And now you've made up your mind I must obviously be a selfish, vindictive creature'

Mrs. B

Sheila

7 'I rather respect you more than I've ever done before'

Ger

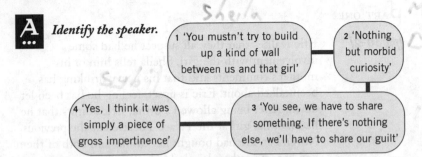

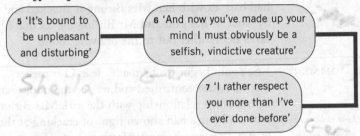

Check your answers on page 76.

B

Consider these issues.

a The significance of the Inspector's comment 'Let's leave offence out of it shall we'.

b Why Daisy Renton wrote in her diary that there'd never be anything as good again for her.

c The stages by which Sheila's attitude towards Gerald changes during this act.

d How the information on Daisy Renton links up with what Mr Birling and Sheila had said about Eva Smith.

e The main reasons why Mrs Birling had refused to help the girl when she appealed to the Brumley Women's Charity Organisation.

f How Mrs Birling justifies refusing to give the girl financial help.

g What the revelation of the girl's refusal to accept stolen money tells us about Mrs Birling and about the girl herself.

h The consequences of Mrs Birling's insistence that all the blame should be placed on the father of the girl's child.

ACT III

PART ONE

[pp. 50–2] Eric realises that they all suspect he had some involvement with the girl. Sheila tells him of his mother's comments and that his heavy drinking has been talked about. Eric is upset, feeling he has been let down. After being allowed a drink, Eric admits that he had met the girl at the Palace Theatre bar the previous November. He had bought her drinks and both of them had become rather drunk. He had insisted on going with her to where she lived, had forced his way in and had had sex with her. Mrs Birling is shocked and upset by what he has said and Mr Birling insists that Sheila takes her mother out to the drawing room.

COMMENT

Look closely at the evidence which shows that the Inspector is now even more firmly in control than before.

Eric's guilt begins to be made clear. Our earlier suspicions are confirmed and we see the unpleasant nature of his relationship with the girl. Mrs Birling's self-confidence had shown signs of cracking at the end of Act Two, and Eric's confession starts to make it crumble. The Inspector now has complete control of the events. His even-handed approach is seen when he overrules Mr Birling and allows Eric to have a drink.

Both Eric and Gerald have met the girl at the Palace Theatre bar and both thought she was different from the prostitutes usually found there. Eric's meeting with the girl in November, some two months after Gerald's affair had ended, neatly fills in the gap in the girl's history.

Eric is careful how he describes what he did, so he simply says 'that's when it happened'.

GLOSSARY

rather far gone very drunk

PART TWO

[pp. 52–3]

Contrast Gerald's behaviour towards the girl with that of Eric.

Eric goes on to detail how he met the girl again two weeks later. She had told him a little about herself and he had told her his name. They had sex again, and had continued to meet but then she told him that she was pregnant. She did not want to marry Eric and he felt that she had treated him like a child. He had given her money, but then she had refused to accept any more.

Birling questions his son about where he had obtained the money and Eric admits he had taken it from his father's office. Before Mr Birling can get any more details, Sheila and Mrs Birling come back into the room.

COMMENT

Details about the girl are vague. Eric does not even mention her name. This uncertainty about her identity is convenient later on in the play when her very existence is questioned.

Eric had told the girl his name. As he was the father of her child it was natural for her to use his name when applying to the Brumley Women's Charity Organisation for help. That, and her unwillingness to accept stolen money, makes Mrs Birling's refusal to help seem even more petty and unjust.

Eric's brutish behaviour towards the girl is closely connected with his excessive drinking.

Eric's language in the all male gathering is coarser than when the ladies are present.

GLOSSARY   **fat old tarts** prostitutes

PART THREE

[pp. 53–6] Mr Birling tells his wife that Eric was responsible for the girl's pregnancy and had stolen money from the office. Eric explains how he had taken the money and claims he had intended to pay it back. Mr Birling begins to plan how he can cover up Eric's fraud. Eric is surprised that the Inspector already knows that the girl had refused to take the money because it was stolen. He is told of Mrs Birling's part in the story, and Eric becomes increasingly emotional. He accuses his mother of killing her own grandchild. The Inspector makes them all listen and he points out to each in turn how they have helped to push the girl towards suicide. He admits that Gerald did at least give the girl some affection and happiness, but stresses that they are all to blame and that they will never forget what they have done. The Inspector's tone becomes prophetic as his final speech foretells what will happen if people do not accept that they must live responsibly as part of a caring community. The Inspector leaves.

Compare Mr Birling's speeches about a man's responsibility (in Act I) with the Inspector's final speech.

COMMENT When Eric reveals his fraud, Mr Birling is immediately aware of the risk of scandal. Once again his first thoughts are to protect himself and his family's good name.

The Inspector's repetition of what each had done to harm the girl is a useful reminder of their weaknesses. It shows that the Inspector's job is nearly over, it leaves them to think back on their part in the girl's death and it builds up the sense of guilt before the Inspector's final speech.

The Inspector's final speech makes a point about responsibility. His references to what will happen in the future make him sound prophetic and suggest he is something more than an ordinary police inspector. It is also used to deliver J.B. Priestley's own strong moral message. Some critics feel he should not have done this, but should have trusted the play to be good enough to carry the message without a sort of sermon being slipped in.

As the Inspector leaves there is a noticeable change of mood. Each member of the Birling family is clearly shaken, and their feeling of self-satisfaction has been destroyed.

PART FOUR

[pp. 56–61]

Mr Birling, convinced there will be a public scandal and that he will not receive the hoped-for knighthood, lays the blame on Eric. Eric says he is as ashamed of his parents as they are of him, but Birling still insists that he and his wife were justified in their behaviour. Sheila is angry at her father. She admits her own guilt and is concerned that her parents do not seem to have learnt anything from what has happened during the evening.

Consider how different characters view the importance of the Inspector's status as a real policeman.

Sheila is struck by the information that the Inspector had arrived just as her father had been stating his view that those who believed people were responsible for others were cranks. She wonders if he was a real policeman. While she is aware that the Inspector's visit had revealed truths about them, her father and mother are excited by the possibility that he might have been an impostor. Sheila and Eric strongly believe that it makes no difference, but their parents disagree and start to list all the things that seemed odd about him. They believe that if he was not a real policeman then a scandal might be avoided. Gerald returns.

COMMENT

Mr Birling clearly feels that Eric is the only one who has behaved in a way which might be seen as directly causing the girl's death. Eric feels that the responsibility is shared equally by them all – Eric's point refers us back to the Inspector's 'chain of events' (p. 14).

Sheila has faced the truth about herself and her actions rather better than her parents have done. She is amazed and disappointed that there has been no real change in their attitudes. Like Eric, she sees no importance in whether the Inspector was a real policeman or not; for her the important thing is that his visit should make them think about, and accept, their responsibilities.

Birling sees the confessions they have made as rash and weak behaviour. He can excuse his own admissions since he feels he only sacked the girl for what anyone would accept as good business reasons.

Birling reverts to the ideas he had expressed to Gerald and Eric in Act I, dismissing, as unstable and dangerous political radicals, anyone who expresses humanitarian feelings.

PART FIVE

[pp. 61–72]

Note the way Gerald and then Mr Birling collect evidence which casts doubt on the identity of the Inspector.

Mr and Mrs Birling keep Sheila from telling Gerald about the involvement of Eric and Mrs Birling. Gerald tells them that while he was out walking he met a local police sergeant who has told him that there is no Inspector Goole or anyone like him. Mr Birling telephones his friend, the Chief Constable, who confirms their suspicion that there is no Inspector Goole. Birling and his wife regain their confidence, convinced that the whole thing has been a trick played on them by someone who doesn't like them. Sheila and Eric remain troubled by their sense of guilt. They feel none of them can escape from the truth that a girl has died and that they were all responsible for her death. Mr Birling again turns on Eric, and is now more concerned with Eric's theft from the firm than with the fate of the girl.

It is Gerald who casts doubt on whether they have really all been involved with the same girl. They have all

behaved cruelly towards a girl, but it might not have
been the same girl. He questions whether the
photographs might have been of different girls and
even wonders whether the story of a girl committing
suicide wasn't simply used to shock them into making
damaging admissions. This leads him to questioning
whether there is a dead girl at all. He telephones the
Infirmary, and learns that no-one has been taken
there after drinking disinfectant. Birling is greatly
relieved, and Mrs Birling congratulates Gerald on
how clever he has been. Sheila and Eric do not join in
the celebrations. They cannot forget what has
happened. These two know that things can never be
quite as they were before and they have learnt
something which will change the way they behave in
the future.

Think about how
their reactions
make Sheila and
Eric different from
the others.

Gerald tries to persuade Sheila to take back the ring,
but she feels she needs time to think. As Mr Birling
tries to make a joke about what has happened, the
telephone rings. He answers it and is told that a police
inspector is on his way to the house to make enquiries
about a young girl's suicide.

COMMENT

It is Gerald who first brings some proof that the Inspector was not a member of the local police force. Gerald uses the uncertainty about the girl's name, and the fact that no-one else saw the photograph shown to any one character, to suggest that there might have been several different girls – one girl that Mr Birling sacked from his factory, one girl that Sheila had had sacked from Milwards, one that Gerald had an affair with and one who was made pregnant by Eric and who probably tried to get help from Mrs Birling.

Mr and Mrs Birling join Gerald in eagerly trying to improve their own situation by discrediting the Inspector. Emphasis is placed on the idea that it has all been a trick, so reducing the seriousness of the admissions they have all made.

The final telephone call was described by Stephen Potter as 'the best coup de theatre of the year'. Consider your view.

Eric and Sheila do not share the relief felt by the others. They have been so deeply affected by the evening's events that the truth of the Inspector's identity makes no difference to them. They cannot forget what they have done.

The telephone call at the end reopens the question of the Inspector's identity. It also leaves the audience wondering whether it will be the same Inspector who comes to question them and how events will progress this time round.

GLOSSARY

moonshine nonsense

an elaborate sell a complicated confidence trick

A
Identify the speaker.

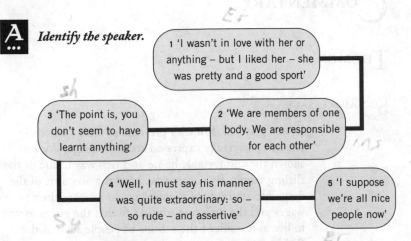

1 'I wasn't in love with her or anything – but I liked her – she was pretty and a good sport'

3 'The point is, you don't seem to have learnt anything'

2 'We are members of one body. We are responsible for each other'

4 'Well, I must say his manner was quite extraordinary: so – so rude – and assertive'

5 'I suppose we're all nice people now'

Identify the person(s) 'to whom' this comment refers.

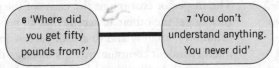

6 'Where did you get fifty pounds from?'

7 'You don't understand anything. You never did'

Check your answers on page 76.

B
Consider these issues.

a How Eric's story completes the pattern of events leading to the girl's death.

b What Mr and Mrs Birling's concern over the stolen money tells us about them.

c The way that Eric's information about the girl ties her in with the girl that Gerald met and the girl who asked Mrs Birling for help.

d How Eric had managed to take the money from his father's office without being caught.

e Which details of the Inspector's final speech contradict views earlier expressed by Mr Birling.

f The way the suspicion that Inspector Goole was not a real policeman develops.

g The reasons why Birling reacts as he does to the possibility that the Inspector was a hoaxer.

h Your reaction to the information Birling receives when he answers the telephone at the end of the play.

PART THREE

COMMENTARY

THEMES

SOCIAL MESSAGE

In this play, J.B. Priestley presents us with a sincerely felt and powerfully expressed social message. We are shown the comfortable home and rich way of life of the Birling family. By contrast we have the accounts of the desperate attempts of the workers to increase their poor wages and the drab and sordid life that the girl is forced to live as a result of the actions of people such as the Birlings.

Consider how we see Priestley's compassion reflected in the play.

The Inspector champions the cause of the poor, and tries to get the others to accept that all people share a common humanity and so are all part of an interdependent community. This message does seem to get through to Sheila and Eric. Sheila is ready to accept and demonstrate this feeling of compassion, but her father simply dismisses the idea of a community, in which responsibility and guilt are shared, as the foolish mutterings of a socialist crank.

MORALITY

As the play progresses, the Inspector's point is put across more and more forcefully. Each character's involvement with Eva Smith/Daisy Renton adds to the Inspector's argument, and he becomes not only a spokesman for the disadvantaged but a voice for the conscience which the Birlings and Gerald seem to lack! The characters, especially the older ones, are increasingly shown to be hiding behind an appearance of respectability which has no foundation in any true sense of morality. The Inspector points out what would

Draw up a list of morally sound and/or morally unacceptable actions for each character.

happen if injustice and inequality were allowed to
continue unchecked. His increasingly missionary tone
reaches its peak when J.B. Priestley's political message is
thundered out in the Inspector's final speech. This
exaggerated oratorical style (see hyperbole in Literary
Terms) might not be acceptable if J.B. Priestley had not
gradually built up the mysterious and prophetic aspects
of the Inspector's character.

POLITICAL VIEW

*You might consider
which modern
politicians, or
political parties,
seem to stress ideas
of community.*

We are never given a clear set of political policies but
J.B. Priestley does make the general point that all of us
have a share in the responsibility for what happens in
our society, that we have a duty of care to others. We
see that the sense of respectability with which the
characters surround themselves does not stand up to
close examination. The way that the older characters
remain unmoved and immovable, uncaring for anyone
but themselves, is one of the horrors of the play. Each
of the revelations has deepened the lesson they should
be learning but they refuse to take any notice. We are
left wondering whether our society today is any less
likely to survive a similarly close examination. Are we
any better in our everyday dealings with other people
than the Birlings?

RESPONSIBILITY

Most of the characters have a narrow view of what it
means to be responsible, but the Inspector provides us
with a much broader one. Mr Birling is a business man
and as such he feels his responsibility is to make a
success of his business, which means making as much
profit as possible even if that means being harsh in his
dealings with those who work for him. As a family man
he sees that he has a responsibility to provide for the

*Think about
which of the
characters you
would say behaved
most irresponsibly.*

material needs of his family, yet it is clear that Eric does not see him as the kind of father to whom he could turn when in trouble. Mrs Birling accepts her responsibility as chairwoman of the Women's Charity Organisation, but only sees a responsibility to help those that she feels are deserving of help. Sheila belatedly recognises that as a powerful customer she has an obligation not to let her personal feelings and ill-temper lead to misery for people who have no power. Eric has little sense of responsibility. He drinks far more than is good for him and he forces the girl into a relationship which has disastrous consequences. He attempts to help her by stealing from his father. Gerald shows some sense of responsibility when he rescues the girl from the unwelcome attentions of another man, feeds her and finds her somewhere to live. Yet he gives in to his own desire for personal pleasure and eventually abandons the girl without knowing, or very much caring, what happens to her.

The Inspector's role is to shake these people up and to make them aware of that broader view of responsibility which J.B. Priestley felt was essential if the world was ever going to learn from its mistakes and become a place where everyone has the right to be treated fairly.

LOVE

The play presents a variety of thoughts about love, the nature of love and different people's interpretation of love. Sheila and Gerald appear to be in love; they have just announced their engagement and seem happy enough contemplating a future dedicated to each other. After each of them has confessed to their shameful behaviour towards Eva Smith/Daisy Renton Sheila realises that they do not really know each other well and that trust is an essential ingredient in a loving relationship.

Mr Birling's remark about the engagement of his daughter bringing the two family firms into a closer working relationship, gives us an indication of his attitude towards love and marriage. He sees marriage as a convenient way of progressing up the social and economic ladder. This makes us wonder whether love played any real part in his marriage to the socially superior Sybil Birling and whether her coldness to others, including her own children, does not have its roots in a loveless marriage.

Consider what evidence there is to suggest that the girl loved Gerald Croft.

Both Gerald and Eric have been involved with the girl, yet each of them denies that they loved her – their relationships were prompted by physical attraction. The girl had taken up with Eric out of necessity, but she does, however, seem to have felt a genuine love for Gerald. Gerald's ending of the affair may be seen as being callous in view of her love for him.

The Inspector preaches a form of love, not too dissimilar to that preached by Christ when he instructed his followers to love one another as much as they love themselves. This form of love is the true 'charity', and is something which appears quite alien to women such as Mrs Birling who bask in the glory of volunteering their time to 'charity' while being devoid of any true charity in their hearts.

TIME

J.B. Priestley wrote the play for an audience just coming out of the horrors of the Second World War, yet he set his play in 1912, two years before the start of the First World War and this brings us to a consideration of J.B. Priestley's use of time as an element of his plays. At the end of the play we are left with a sense that the events are going to start all over again. We wonder whether things will be different and how the characters will behave.

Ouspensky's theory

Think about whether any of the characters changed sufficiently to escape into a new life.

J.B. Priestley became fascinated by theories about the nature of time. Put simply, most of us see time as a straight line going from one point to another in a continuous sequence. J.B. Priestley read P.D. Ouspensky's book *A New Model of the Universe* in which it was suggested that when we die we re-enter our life once more from the beginning. We are born again in the same house to the same parents and continue to repeat all the events of our life just as before. This cycle of identical lives would go on being repeated if we changed nothing of significance. If, however, we improved in some spiritual way, we could convert the circle into a spiral of events that would, if we continued to make significant improvements, eventually open the way for us to escape from the repetitions and into a new life in which we did not repeat our mistakes.

Dunne's theory

Consider whether any of the characters, given the chance, would have changed their past actions.

J.W. Dunne was another time theorist who influenced J.B. Priestley. Dunne laid out the idea that you could be given the gift of seeing forward in time as well as looking back. This would mean that, just as you can look back and see what actions led to your present situation, you could look forward and see the consequences of your actions. So, if you wished, you could change those actions and so avoid the consequences.

An Inspector Calls contains elements of these time theories. The Inspector, arriving before the suicide is a reality, offers each a chance to see the consequences, to change the future, to break the circle. Eric and Sheila seem prepared to take that opportunity to face up to their past actions and to improve themselves, but the others do not. The reflections on the past, and the possibilities of the future highlight the importance of caring for others, of taking responsibility for our actions and of considering the consequences of them. The

Consider which of the characters might see the Inspector as a force for good and which might see him as a power for evil.

Inspector's knowledge of events, apparently before they happen, his steady revelation of the characters' pasts and their links to the dead girl over a two-year period gives him a mystical, unworldly quality – what J.C. Trewin in his review of the play in the *Observer* in 1946 called 'the angel with the flaming sword'. His departure leaves the characters free to decide their future, while at the end we are left to wonder how they will cope with reliving the close scrutiny of their dealings with others when the cycle starts all over again.

By setting the play in 1912 and presenting it to a later audience, J.B. Priestley has covered an era which includes both World Wars. The failure of the older characters to learn anything reflects the failure of generations to learn from the mistakes of the recent past. There is dramatic irony (see Literary Terms) in that characters talk of hopes for peace and prosperity, but we know these will not happen. By 1945 J.B. Priestley was hoping that the second time around the world might learn from past mistakes and we might see such hopes realised if we, the audience, can accept the challenge to be caring and socially aware.

STRUCTURE

This play follows the tradition of what is known as a well-made play. It has a plot in which the action flows smoothly and all the parts fit together precisely, rather like parts of a jigsaw puzzle. As a result the characters and the audience move from a state of ignorance to a state of knowledge. J.B. Priestley wanted his play to have a uniformity of manner and tone with one situation rapidly moving on to the next. He felt that he could best achieve this by writing quickly, and indeed he completed this play in a week. The unity of time and place is achieved by the events all taking place in the dining room and the action running continuously through all the three acts. Even when there is a break between acts where an interval might be placed, the start of the next act takes us to the same point in time at which we had left the action.

The action is taken forward by the Inspector's questioning of each character in turn. Their reasons for entering or leaving are always plausible and always allow some new aspect of the plot to be introduced or something mentioned earlier to be developed. The play is built up in a series of episodes and each character has either a leading or supporting role in each of these episodes, even in their absence. Gerald's decision to go for a walk, for example, means that he can alter the course of events after the Inspector's departure, while Eric's similar absence allows his involvement with Eva Smith/Daisy Renton to be explored in a way that it could not be if he were present. Each new revelation, prompted by the Inspector's careful use of the photograph or information from the diary, adds to the overall picture of those two crucial years in the girl's life. Each part fits together and helps to complete the jigsaw of events and involvements. As the pattern develops the audience is able to predict what will happen next.

Look at the celluloid summary on pp. 16–17 of these Notes; try to devise your own summary for Eva/Daisy's life or for the events of the evening.

J.B. Priestley brings about quite subtle changes of mood. The play begins in a mood of high celebration, but after the Inspector's entrance, the other characters have little reason for self-congratulation and the mood becomes more sombre, even threatening. By the time the Inspector delivers his final speech the mood has become one that promises real danger for the future. The relief that is felt when the Inspector is seemingly shown up as a hoaxer and no evidence of a suicide can be found is shattered by the dramatic telephone call. J.B. Priestley even uses stage directions (see Literary

Terms) to suggest how the lighting effects can reflect the mood. He orders a 'pink and intimate' use of lights for the party which changes to 'brighter and harder' when the Inspector's investigation begins.

Although the action and the time span of the play is realistic, J.B. Priestley throws in two twists at the end. Firstly we have the problem of who the Inspector really was: a trickster determined to make fools of them or some sort of avenging spirit come to make them see the evil of their ways? The second twist is the time-release mechanism when the telephone call interrupts and takes them back to relive the events. It is this which allows the possibility that the Inspector was a real policeman who has slipped out of real time and will return. If they fail to learn from their experiences and are 'ready to go on in the same old way' (p. 71) the Inspector's threat of 'fire and blood and anguish' (p. 56) will become their reality.

THE INSPECTOR

Mysterious
Imposing
Sombre
Determined
Calm

The word 'inspector' suggests someone who looks closely at things, and this is his role in the events of the play. The name 'Goole' is the same as the seaport town of Goole at the mouth of the River Humber, and perhaps suggests that the Inspector is going to fish for information, to trawl through the lives and deeply hidden secrets of the other characters. The name also sounds like ghoul – someone with a morbid interest in death, a spirit which is said to take fresh life from corpses, and it is certainly arguable that the Inspector's existence is a result of the girl's death.

Described as creating 'an impression of massiveness, solidity and purposefulness', the Inspector grows as the stories of each character are revealed. He remains solid and intact as each of them breaks down, and nothing the others can do or say distracts him from his purpose.

He arrives just after Mr Birling has been setting out his view of life: that every man must only look out for himself. The Inspector's role is to show that this is not the case. Throughout the play he demonstrates how people are responsible for how they affect the lives of others and his views are summed up in his visionary and dramatic final speech. It is the Inspector who makes things happen. Without him none of the secrets would ever have come into the open. He seems to know what each character has done, and his probing questions leave them to confess in their own way. From the moment of his arrival he seems different. His sombre appearance and the news he brings are a contrast with the happy and elegant air of celebration. Despite the importance in the local community of people like Gerald and the Birlings, he controls the development of events: who will speak and when; who may or may not leave; who will or will not see the photograph. He even seems to control what people say. Sheila, who has commented on his mysterious character, tells Gerald 'Somehow he makes you' (p. 37). The Inspector has Eva Smith's diary and a letter. From these he has built up a picture of her life and character. He uses this information, with constant reminders of the horrific death she has suffered, to force them to face up to what they have done. He links the series of wrongs done to the girl so that they are seen to build up to pressure which forces her to her last desperate act.

The way he uses the information he has creates an impression of someone who is both an outsider and an all-knowing creature. This makes him appear mysterious and powerful. Yet J.B. Priestley can only use him as a catalyst, as someone who creates the possibility for others to face up to what they have done. They must decide for themselves whether to change or not. He is a character who represents J.B. Priestley's strong moral view. His comments show a compassion which extends to those who recognise the wrong they have done. He does not forgive what they have done, but when they freely admit their faults he allows them to see that they can find forgiveness through future good behaviour. This moral dimension makes him different from an ordinary policeman. He is more concerned with right and wrong than with what is or is not legal. His lack of fear or favour, his determined questioning and control of events may be what is expected of a policeman, but towards the end of the play it is those same qualities (identified by Mrs Birling as rudeness) which fuel suspicions about him. His approach has been perhaps too abrasive, and he is clearly someone for whom social conventions count for nothing when weighed against the desire for truth and justice.

MR BIRLING

Wealthy business man

Involved in local politics

Pompous

Self-important

Unsophisticated

Bully

Mr Birling is a successful business man who has been active in local politics and has had the honour of being Lord Mayor. He is a magistrate and has hopes of being given a knighthood which will make him socially closer to Sir George and Lady Croft. He is described as a 'heavy-looking rather portentous man'. His size perhaps helps to give him the threatening appearance suggested by that description. He is self-confident, but his upbringing makes him less socially aware and gracious than either his wife or Gerald Croft. He sees the engagement of Gerald and Sheila as being good for business and later it is business interests which most affect his attitude to Eric's theft of money from the firm.

His view of his own importance leads him:

- To try to use his social status to intimidate the Inspector
- To try to impose his will and authority on Eric and Sheila
- To be concerned about the effect of a scandal on his chances of a knighthood

It is central to the play that his attitude that 'a man has to mind his own business and look after his own' (p. 10) is discredited by the confessions that the Inspector draws out. Yet he does not change his views or attitudes over the course of the play. Though he reveals more of his contempt for weakness and his anger at the foolish behaviour of others, he cannot see that his actions towards the girl were wrong, and we feel that if the events were repeated he would still feel justified in sacking the girl. He feels this was, and still is, the right attitude for a man of business. He sees nothing strange in wanting to protect Sheila from the unpleasantness of the girl's life and death, yet feels no guilt at not having protected the girl herself.

After the Inspector has gone he simply wants things to return to the way they were. He cannot understand Sheila's and Eric's insistence that there is something to be learnt, and he is relieved and triumphant when he feels that scandal has been avoided and everything is all right. Despite his self-centred and unrepentant attitude it is possible to feel some sympathy for him at the end of the play when his relief that the incident is over and done with is shattered by the telephone call. Perhaps we can feel this because J.B. Priestley lets us see someone who is so blindly wrong and never as really in control of events as he would like himself, and others, to think.

Mrs Birling

Cold
Unfeeling
Socially correct
Self-important
Out-of-touch with reality of life

Mrs Birling is described as a 'rather cold woman and her husband's social superior'. Her coldness and lack of conscience make her unsympathetic, while her keen awareness of the rules of polite behaviour (shown, for example, in the way she rebukes her husband for his comment about the quality of the meal) makes her seem out of touch with what really matters. Her lack of understanding of how other people live is shown in her snobbish comments about 'a girl of that sort' (p. 47) and in her unwillingness to believe the girl's reasons for refusing to take the stolen money or marry the foolish young man responsible for her pregnancy. Her lack of understanding even extends to her family as she has been quite unaware of her own son's heavy drinking.

She remains untouched by the Inspector's questioning, and refuses to see how her actions could have been responsible for the girl's death. We can clearly see that her refusal to help the girl could easily have been what finally led to her suicide, yet it is only when she realises that Eric was the child's father and so her actions had resulted in the death of her own grandchild that she

begins to show any signs of weakening. The speed
with which she recovers after the Inspector's departure
emphasises how cold and unsympathetic a character
she is.

She can be seen as hypocritical because:

- She claims to be shocked by Eric's drinking and the
  talk of immoral relationships with the girl, yet she
  cannot bear not to hear Eric's confession
- She is quite content to lay all the blame on the father
  of the child. When it becomes clear that the young
  man is her son, she is not prepared to own up to her
  comments until Sheila brings them into the open
- Earlier on she had condemned Gerald's 'disgusting
  affair' (p. 38) but seems quite willing to forget about
  it once the threat of shared blame seems to have
  been withdrawn

There is no sense of relief that her selfish actions have
not been the cause of tragedy. The glowing thanks and
praise that she lavishes on Gerald for the clever way he
appears to have settled things reflect her desire to
remain untouched by outside events and to maintain
the appearance of respectability.

SHEILA BIRLING

Sheila is described as 'a pretty girl in her early twenties,
very pleased with life and rather excited'. Early on
in the play she is playful and rather self-centred,
enjoying the attention and importance that her
engagement is bringing her. Her curiosity when she
finds her father, Eric and Gerald with the Inspector
is at first superficial, but she soon shows a sensitive
side to her nature and is moved by the news of the
girl's death. Her own happiness seems almost unfair
to her and, even before she has any idea of her own

Young
Pretty
Lively
Selfish
Ill-tempered
Later sympathetic,
repentant and
caring

part in the dead girl's story, she seems truly interested. Unlike her father, she responds to the girl as a person, not as cheap labour. She is prepared to criticise her father and shows that though she is foolish and selfish, she has the potential to change.

When Sheila realises that her own jealousy and bad temper had led to the girl losing her job at the shop, she is genuinely sorry. Yet we also see that her sorrow is linked to her feeling of regret that she will not be able to go back to a favourite shop, and so her streak of selfishness is still there. By the end of Act I, Sheila is already aware of the influence of the Inspector and is beginning to question how deep his knowledge goes. She warns Gerald 'Of course he knows. And I hate to think how much he knows that we don't know yet' (p. 26).

Sheila grows stronger and more sympathetic as the play goes on. She is obviously upset by Gerald's confession, but is strong enough to cope with it and even to acknowledge that she is impressed by Gerald's honesty. Her realisation that honesty and truth really matter shows that she is capable of learning and changing. She has begun to have some understanding of what the Inspector is doing so that she is able to see the world, and her responsibility, according to his values instead of those of her family. This is why she can see the trap her mother's arrogance is creating, and why she tries to stop her mother from exposing and condemning the child's father. It is only Sheila and Eric, the two youngest and 'more impressionable' (p. 30) characters who feel everyone needs to learn something from what has happened. Sheila does seem to have learnt something and to have changed, and we feel that her future attitude to others will be more caring, self-controlled and responsible.

ERIC BIRLING

Awkward
Immature
Thoughtless
Selfish
Drunkard
Thief

Unlike his sister, Sheila, Eric is awkward 'not quite at ease, half shy, half assertive'. He does not seem to have his father's affection or approval. He is kept out of the information about his father's possible knighthood, and when he really needed help he felt his father was 'not the kind of father a chap could go to when he's in trouble' (p. 54). He drinks too much, has forced his way into the girl's home, has made the girl pregnant and stolen money.

Like Sheila, he feels sympathy for Eva Smith as soon as he hears how Mr Birling had sacked her. When he has to admit how he behaved towards her he has a stronger sense of guilt than the others because the consequences of what he did are so much worse. It is not surprising that he turns violently on his mother when he learns how she had refused to help the girl. He curses his mother and accuses her of killing both the girl and the child. He had been rude to his father earlier and his rudeness to his parents increases the more he drinks. One can imagine how frightening he might have seemed to the girl when he was drunk – 'in that state when a chap easily turns nasty' (p. 52). His immaturity shows in his casual attitude towards his relationship with the girl whom he regarded as a 'good sport' (p. 52) although she treated him like a child. He appears to have learnt very little from his privileged education.

Yet he is one of the young ones who has been impressed by the Inspector. He wants his parents to admit their mistakes as freely as he has admitted his. Though he is not a particularly pleasant character, we may feel that he has learnt a lesson, he is sincerely ashamed of his behaviour and he is capable of changing for the better.

GERALD CROFT

Gerald is the son of Birling's rival industrialist, Sir George Croft. He has the self-confidence of someone who is at ease wherever he is or whoever he is with. He is polite and tactful with Mr and Mrs Birling. Being about thirty, he is older than Sheila and Eric whose parents treat Gerald as something of an equal. He is trusted with the secret of Arthur Birling's possible knighthood. Gerald's views on the way a business should be run, how workers should be treated and the importance of profit are all in line with those of Mr Birling, and he supports the reasoning with which Mr Birling justifies Eva Smith's sacking from the firm.

Self-assured
Well mannered
Business man
Sense of chivalry
but is morally
weak

When he first meets Daisy Renton he saves her from the awkward situation with Alderman Meggarty and sets out to help her. His good intentions, however, go astray. He had found Daisy attractive from the start, and he allowed his feelings to develop. He felt affection for her but admits that her feelings for him were stronger than his feelings for her. He felt guilty about only being able to offer her temporary help and when he left her he gave her money to help her to start a new life. The fact that he 'Made her happy for a time' (p. 56) allows us to feel some sympathy for him. His regret for the way he used her is genuine, but he does not have the same deep response as Sheila to the Inspector's message. He acts on his suspicions, and as a result he is the one who begins the chain of events leading to the feeling of certainty that Goole had been an impostor.

MINOR CHARACTERS

Edna

Edna, the maid, appears only briefly. Her presence strengthens the impression of the solidity, privilege and wealth which the Birlings enjoy. It is Edna, the only one of the working people in the household that we see on stage, who announces the Inspector's arrival.

Eva Smith/ Daisy Renton   The girl remains a mystery. She never appears on stage and we do not know her real name, but the play revolves round the last two years of her life. We know she was pretty enough to make Sheila jealous and to attract the attention of both Gerald and Eric. What we learn about her, her drab life and unpleasant death, contrasts sharply with what we see and learn of the Birling family and Gerald Croft. She worked hard, supported her fellow workers and was kind and gentle. Although she was reduced to earning her living by picking up men in the Palace Theatre bar, she did not seem well suited to that way of life. Her sense of right and wrong prevented her from considering marriage to Eric and protected him from his folly in stealing money from his father's firm. Despite five separate stories, she remains more of a symbol than a real person. She stands for all the people we meet in our everyday lives. J.B. Priestley uses her tragedy to jolt us into thinking about our responsibility towards others. She is the weapon the Inspector uses to try to change the attitudes of the others. His final speech reminds us that 'One Eva Smith has gone – but there are millions and millions and millions of Eva Smiths and John Smiths still left with us, with their lives, their hopes and fears, their suffering and chance of happiness, all intertwined with our lives, and what we think and say and do' (p. 56).

The realism of Priestley's language

The realism of the play, its realistic set and realistic incidents, is reinforced by the realism of the language. The dialogue (see Literary Terms) is, however, grammatically correct and so does not reflect the true patterns of everyday speech in a way that a modem play by Pinter or Potter would. The realism of language is, however, the realism of 1912, and though the language of Edwardian England differs in some respects to what sounds natural today, there are no real problems of communication.

Language helps to reinforce the Inspector's authority.

We are told that the Inspector speaks 'carefully, weightily' and we can see that what he says consists largely of questions and instructions. This helps him to control, direct and develop the plot. His words are often matter of fact, as we would expect from a policeman, but the tone is commanding and even threatening. His final speech uses a quite different sort of language: it is the language of the prophet or the missionary and sounds more like a sermon than the carefully weighed evidence of a policeman. There are times when he produces dramatic results by use of a very short and isolated sentence – or even a single word. At other times he speaks in long sentences which are broken up to produce a rhythm which gives what he says extra emphasis and makes what he says profoundly logical e.g. 'Because what happened to her then may have determined what happened to her afterwards, and what happened to her afterwards may have driven her to suicide'. Those words are followed by the terse comment 'A chain of events' and we can see that the logical sequence links up just like the links of the chain.

There is an emphasis on correct behaviour and good manners – especially in Mrs Birling's speeches – yet the Inspector frequently interrupts characters who are not going in the direction he wishes them to go in. The interruptions balance the often lively dialogues and monologues which carry the story-line forward, but the Inspector's interruptions and his indifference to the nicer points of polite behaviour make him stand apart from the others every bit as much as does his precise and incisive language.

The language used by each character helps us to create a clearer picture of them.

Mr Birling, we are told, is 'rather provincial in his speech' and he frequently speaks in a rather bullying and forceful manner which at times mirrors what he felt was expected of a solid, middle-class Edwardian without being really convincing. His comments about a possible knighthood and his congratulations to the cook are not in keeping with correct behaviour.

Gerald Croft, on the other hand, is inevitably careful and correct in what he says. For example, cleverly freeing Mr Birling from his social error about the good meal by his careful comment about being one of the family, and later using a euphemism (see Literary Terms) instead of saying prostitute. His one lapse is in his description of Alderman Meggarty, and that may reflect the anger he felt as a result of his care for Daisy Renton.

Sheila and Eric are less restrained and their use of slang expressions such as 'squiffy' shock their parents and show up the generation gap as clearly as do their bitter comments on their parents' behaviour.

Much of the play's success depends upon the dramatic irony (see Literary Terms) which J.B. Priestley creates. We see this in the mistaken view that Mr Birling has about the future, his faith in technology and belief in peace. We can guess from this that his view of a man's responsibility will be equally wrong. Similarly, when Sheila has worked out that Eric might well be the father of Eva Smith's child, there is irony in that Mrs Birling has not realised it and is unwittingly demanding that an example should be made of none other than her own son.

*Priestley uses
irony in more
than one way.*

Perhaps there is a different sort of irony (see Literary Terms) in the fact that the Inspector has been talking as much to us, the audience, as to the characters. We have to ask ourselves whether we are in a position to judge what has happened when we are probably as guilty of acting irresponsibly and unkindly as anyone on stage! This irony strengthens our feeling that J.B. Priestley's type of socialism is not so much about politics but about caring and even, perhaps, about love.

PART FOUR

STUDY SKILLS

HOW TO USE QUOTATIONS

One of the secrets of success in writing essays is the
way you use quotations. There are five basic principles:

- Put inverted commas at the beginning and end of the
  quotation
- Write the quotation exactly as it appears in the
  orginal
- Do not use a quotation that repeats what you have
  just written
- Use the quotation so that it fits into your sentence
- Keep the quotation as short as possible

Quotations should be used to develop the line of
thought in your essays.

Your comment should not duplicate what is in your
quotation. For example:

**Gerald Croft tells the Inspector that he first met Daisy Renton in
the bar of the local theatre the previous spring, 'I met her first,
sometime in March last year, in the stalls bar at the Palace'.**

Far more effective is to write:

**Gerald Croft says that he first met Daisy Renton 'in the stalls bar
at the Palace' which is the local music hall theatre.**

Always lay out the lines as they appear in the text. For
example:

The revelation leads Eric to turn savagely on his mother:

**'... yes, and you killed her – and the child she'd have had too –
my child – your own grandchild – you killed them both – damn
you, damn you –'**

The most sophisticated way of using the writer's words
is to embed them into your sentence:

**Gerald, seeing that Alderman Meggarty was 'half-drunk and
goggle-eyed', wanted to rescue Daisy Renton from him.**

Using quotations in this way, you are demonstrating the
ability to use text as evidence to support your ideas.

Everyone writes differently. Work through the suggestions given here and adapt the advice to suit your own style and interests. This will improve your essay-writing skills and allow your personal voice to emerge.

The following points indicate in ascending order the skills of essay writing:

- Picking out one or two facts about the story and adding the odd detail
- Writing about the text by retelling the story
- Retelling the story and adding a quotation here and there
- Organising an answer which explains what is happening in the text and giving quotations to support what you write

....

- Writing in such a way as to show that you have thought about the intentions of the writer of the text and that you understand the techniques used
- Writing at some length, giving your viewpoint on the text and commenting by picking out details to support your views
- Looking at the text as a work of art, demonstrating clear critical judgement and explaining to the reader of your essay how the enjoyment of the text is assisted by literary devices, linguistic effects and psychological insights; showing how the text relates to the time when it was written

The dotted line above represents the division between lower and higher level grades. Higher-level performance begins when you start to consider your response as a reader of the text. The highest level is reached when you offer an enthusiastic personal response and show how this piece of literature is a product of its time.

Coursework essay

Set aside an hour or so at the start of your work to plan what you have to do.

- List all the points you feel are needed to cover the task. Collect page references of information and quotations that will support what you have to say. A helpful tool is the highlighter pen: this saves painstaking copying and enables you to target precisely what you want to use.

- Focus on what you consider to be the main points of the essay. Try to sum up your argument in a single sentence, which could be the closing sentence of your essay. Depending on the essay title, it could be a statement about a character: Sheila Birling is one of the more sensitive characters in *An Inspector Calls*, as she clearly becomes fully aware of her responsibility and, despite her parents, she is prepared to change her selfish ways; an opinion about setting: I believe that the heavy comfort of the Birling family's dining room accurately reflects that family's comfortable sense of contentment with life; or a judgement on a theme: I think that the main theme of *An Inspector Calls* is responsibility, because the Inspector's questioning reveals the irresponsible behaviour of each of the other characters in turn.

- Make a short essay plan. Use the first paragraph to introduce the argument you wish to make. In the following paragraphs develop this argument with details, examples and other possible points of view. Sum up your argument in the last paragraph. Check you have answered the question.

- Write the essay, remembering all the time the central point you are making.

- On completion, go back over what you have written to eliminate careless errors and improve expression. Read it aloud to yourself, or, if you are feeling more confident, to a relative or friend.

If you can, try to type your essay, using a word processor. This will allow you to correct and improve your writing without spoiling its appearance.

Examination essay

The essay written in an examination often carries more marks than the coursework essay even though it is written under considerable time pressure.

In the revision period build up notes on various aspects of the text you are using. Fortunately, in acquiring this set of York Notes on *An Inspector Calls*, you have made a prudent beginning! York Notes are set out to give you vital information and help you to construct your personal overview of the text.

Make notes with appropriate quotations about the key issues of the set text. Go into the examination knowing your text and having a clear set of opinions about it.

In most English Literature examinations, you can take in copies of your set books. This is an enormous advantage although it may lull you into a false sense of security. Beware! There is simply not enough time in an examination to read the book from scratch.

In the examination

- Read the question paper carefully and remind yourself what you have to do.
- Look at the questions on your set texts to select the one that most interests you and mentally work out the points you wish to stress.
- Remind yourself of the time available and how you are going to use it.
- Briefly map out a short plan in note form that will keep your writing on track and illustrate the key argument you want to make.
- Then set about writing it.
- When you have finished, check through to eliminate errors.

To summarise, these are the keys to success:
- **Know the text**
- **Have a clear understanding of and opinions on the storyline, characters, setting, themes and writer's concerns**
- **Select the right material**
- **Plan and write a clear response, continually bearing the question in mind**

SAMPLE ESSAY PLAN

A typical essay question on *An Inspector Calls* is followed by a sample essay plan in note form. This does not present the only answer to the question, merely one answer. Do not be afraid to include your own ideas, and leave out some of those in the sample! Remember that quotations are essential to prove and illustrate the points you make.

To what extent can Gerald Croft be held responsible for the death of Eva Smith/Daisy Renton?

Such a question anticipates a wide-ranging response. Let us suppose that you feel that Gerald does bear considerable responsibility for the death of the girl. To answer the question 'to what extent' you will have to put his role in context.

Part 1   A description of Gerald Croft, his background and his relationship with the Birling family.

Part 2   How his relationship with the girl is revealed, his desire to keep the relationship secret, where he met the girl, why he noticed her, how the relationship developed, and how the relationship ended.

Part 3   An examination of his motives – to rescue a pretty girl in trouble, to offer food and shelter to someone who was vulnerable. His reaction to the affection that the girl's gratitude generated. Your decision on whether his motives were honourable a) when he first met the girl, b) when he offered her accommodation, c) when he made her his mistress and d) when he left her.

Part 4   Where Gerald's association with the girl fits in with the girl's contact with the other characters: what each had done: how the links of the chain fit together.

Part 5   The girl had been happy with Gerald, so he had given her something worthwhile in her life. How Gerald's treatment contrasts with the treatment of others, how he improved the quality of her life. But that, after he left her, her life had been so much worse.

Part 6:   That Gerald might be the only one that even the
Conclusion   Inspector admits made her happy for a time, but he let her down as much as anyone else, perhaps more so since he gave her a little happiness and then took it away, leaving her at the mercy of people like Eric – a younger version of Alderman Meggarty. Gerald's support of Mr Birling over the sacking of the girl from the factory, his lead in disproving the authenticity of the Inspector and his telephone call to the Infirmary, his willingness to believe that since there was no dead girl then there was 'no need to feel guilty or troubled' – shown by his instant request to Sheila to take back the ring, all suggest that he has not learnt a lesson and must take at least an equal share of the guilt.

This is by no means an exhaustive or definitive answer to the question. However, looked at in conjunction with the general notes on Essay Writing, it does show you the way your mind should be working in order to produce a reasonably thorough essay.

Make a plan as shown above and attempt these questions.

1 Which of the characters is most affected by the events of the evening?

2 How is *An Inspector Calls* different from a typical detective thriller?

3 Examine the evidence to decide whether Eva Smith and Daisy Renton are indeed one and the same person.

4 How does the play show up the contrast between the philosophies of Arthur Birling and Inspector Goole?

5 What aspects of British society does the play criticise?

PART FIVE

CULTURAL CONNECTIONS

BROADER PERSPECTIVES

Think of other plays or novels, in which characters are led to ever more tragic revelations.

Any moment in time can be seen as one link in a 'chain of events' that goes back as well as forward in time. Through the device of a mysterious time-shift, the central event of the plot of *An Inspector Calls* – the girl's suicide – is introduced before it actually happens. Into the opening scene of a comfortable and complacent family happily celebrating an engagement, the Inspector's shrewd and determined questions introduce a strong sense of unease. A shocking catalogue of cruelty and indifference for others is revealed, offering each character a choice between condemnation or a chance of redemption. Those ideas of how far we are able to determine our own destiny are also explored in J.B. Priestley's play *Dangerous Corner* (in *J.B. Priestley's Six Plays*, Heinemann, 1979 – first published as an individual play in 1932).

Try to think of other texts that use distortion of time for effect.

If you wanted to explore J.B. Priestley's time theories in greater detail, you might also like to read his plays *I Have Been Here Before* (Heinemann, 1948 – first published 1937) and *Time and the Conways* (in *J.B. Priestley's Six Plays*, Heinemann, 1979 – first published as an individual play in 1937). His plays are regularly included in the programmes of local theatre companies and are well worth a visit. You might like to look at how other people have explored time. Charles Dickens in *A Christmas Carol* (O.U.P., 1995 – first published 1843) shows the miser Scrooge given the opportunity both to look back on his past life and forward to the future so that he is able to change his ways and so avoid the tragic consequences of his meanness.

Modern films, such as *Back to the Future* (1985), use the idea of intervention by a superior being to bring about a change to the lives of others by affecting what has happened in the past; while *Groundhog Day* (1993) uses the notion of time being circular, though it is condensed into a repetition of one day rather than a repetition of lifetimes!

The BBC televised *An Inspector Calls* in 1981, starring Bernard Hepton as the Inspector. A film of *An Inspector Calls* directed by Guy Hamilton and starring Alastair Sim as the Inspector was made in 1954. Unlike the BBC version the film did not keep to J.B. Priestley's original play, but showed in flashback (see Literary Terms) the various episodes featuring Eva Smith/Daisy Renton. It also had an interesting additional twist at the end, featuring an empty rocking chair, which cast further doubt on the exact nature of J.B. Priestley's mysterious Inspector!

Different directors will have their own approach to a play or a film.

If you want to find out more about the life and times of J.B. Priestley himself, you might like to read Vincent Brome's biography *J.B. Priestley* (Hamish Hamilton, 1988), especially the section dealing with the 'time plays'.

antithesis a direct opposite, contrast. An argument which directly opposes one stated earlier

bombast pompous or inflated language

characternym a name that represents its bearer in some way

colloquialism the use of the kinds of expression and grammar associated with ordinary, everyday speech rather than formal language

coup de theatre a sudden and spectacular turn to events in the plot of a play

dialectic an argument which takes away any doubt and so leads to the discovery of what is true

dialogue speech and conversation between characters

dramatic irony this occurs when the development of the plot allows the audience to possess more information about what is happening than some of the characters have themselves

empathy a kind of sympathy, but stronger: empathy suggests total involvement with the object of sympathy, so that we seem to be inside it for the moment

euphemism unpleasant, embarrassing or frightening facts or words can be concealed behind a 'euphemism' – a word or phrase less blunt or offensive

flashback a word borrowed from films. A sudden jump backwards in time to an earlier episode or scene in the story

genre the term for a type or kind of writing, e.g. poetry, drama and prose which can be sub-divided into such things as love poetry, comedies, science fiction

hyperbole a figure of speech in which emphasis is achieved by exaggeration

irony this consists of saying one thing while you mean another, often through understatement, concealment or indirect statement

monologue lengthy speech by one person

prose all writing not in verse

pun two widely different meanings drawn out of a single word in a witty, and sometimes comic way e.g. in Act II the way 'offence' is used by Mrs Birling to suggest she has been offended, and then used by the Inspector to suggest a crime has been committed

stage directions advice printed in the text of a play giving instructions or information about the movements, gestures and appearance of the actors, or on the special effects required at a particular moment in the action

voice a word sometimes used to denote the author's point of view

Test Yourself (Act I)

A
1 Mr Birling
... 2 The Inspector
3 Mr Birling
4 Sheila
5 Gerald
6 Mr Birling
7 Sheila

Test Yourself (Act II)

A
1 Sheila
... 2 Mrs Birling
3 The Inspector

4 Mrs Birling
5 Sheila
6 Gerald
7 Gerald

Test Yourself (Act III)

A
1 Eric
... 2 The Inspector
3 Sheila
4 Mrs Birling
5 Sheila
6 Eric
7 Mrs Birling

Titles in the York Notes Series

GCSE and equivalent levels (£3.50 each)

Harold Brighouse
Hobson's Choice

Charles Dickens
Great Expectations

Charles Dickens
Hard Times

George Eliot
Silas Marner

William Golding
Lord of the Flies

Thomas Hardy
The Mayor of Casterbridge

Susan Hill
I'm the King of the Castle

Barry Hines
A Kestrel for a Knave

Harper Lee
To Kill a Mockingbird

Arthur Miller
A View from the Bridge

Arthur Miller
The Crucible

George Orwell
Animal Farm

J.B. Priestley
An Inspector Calls

J.D. Salinger
The Catcher in the Rye

William Shakespeare
Macbeth

William Shakespeare
The Merchant of Venice

William Shakespeare
Romeo and Juliet

William Shakespeare
Twelfth Night

George Bernard Shaw
Pygmalion

John Steinbeck
Of Mice and Men

Mildred D. Taylor
Roll of Thunder, Hear My Cry

James Watson
Talking in Whispers

A Choice of Poets

Nineteenth Century Short Stories

Poetry of the First World War

FORTHCOMING TITLES IN THE SERIES

Advanced level (£3.99 each)

Margaret Atwood
The Handmaid's Tale

Jane Austen
Emma

Jane Austen
Pride and Prejudice

William Blake
Poems/Songs of Innocence and Songs of Experience

Emily Brontë
Wuthering Heights

Geoffrey Chaucer
Wife of Bath's Prologue and Tale

Joseph Conrad
Heart of Darkness

Charles Dickens
Great Expectations

F. Scott Fitzgerald
The Great Gatsby

Thomas Hardy
Tess of the D'Urbervilles

Seamus Heaney
Selected Poems

James Joyce
Dubliners

William Shakespeare
Antony and Cleopatra

William Shakespeare
Hamlet

William Shakespeare
King Lear

William Shakespeare
Macbeth

William Shakespeare
Othello

Mary Shelley
Frankenstein

Alice Walker
The Color Purple

John Webster
The Duchess of Malfi

York Notes – the Ultimate Literature Guides

York Notes are recognised as the best literature study guides.
If you have enjoyed using this book and have found it useful, you
can now order others directly from us – simply follow the ordering
instructions below.

HOW TO ORDER

Decide which title(s) you require and then order in one of the following
ways:

Booksellers
All titles available from good bookstores.

By post
List the title(s) you require in the space provided overleaf,
select your method of payment, complete your name and
address details and return your completed order form and
payment to:

> *Addison Wesley Longman Ltd*
> *PO BOX 88*
> *Harlow*
> *Essex CM19 5SR*

By phone
Call our Customer Information Centre on 01279 623923 to
place your order, quoting mail number: HEYN1.

By fax
Complete the order form overleaf, ensuring you fill in your
name and address details and method of payment, and fax it
to us on 01279 414130.

By e-mail
E-mail your order to us on awlhe.orders@awl.co.uk listing
title(s) and quantity required and providing full name and
address details as requested overleaf. Please
quote mail number: HEYN1. Please do not
send credit card details by e-mail.

York Notes Order Form

Titles required:

Quantity	Title/ISBN	Price

Sub total _____

Please add £2.50 postage & packing _____

(*P & P is free for orders over £50*) _____

Total _____

Mail no: HEYN1

Your Name _____

Your Address _____

_____

Postcode _____ Telephone _____

Method of payment

☐ I enclose a cheque or a P/O for £_____ made payable to
Addison Wesley Longman Ltd

☐ Please charge my Visa/Access/AMEX/Diners Club card
Number _____ Expiry Date _____
Signature _____ Date _____

(please ensure that the address given above is the same as for your credit card)

Prices and other details are correct at time of going to press but may change without notice.
All orders are subject to status.

☐ *Please tick this box if you*
would like a complete listing of
Longman Study Guides
(suitable for GCSE and A-level students)

York Press

Longman

Addison
Wesley
Longman